Why I Go
To Church

By
Edgar A. Guest

Verse—

Harbor Lights of Home
The Light of Faith
The Passing Throng
A Heap o' Livin'
Just Folks
The Path to Home
Poems of Patriotism
When Day Is Done
Rhymes of Childhood

Illustrated—

All That Matters

Gift Books—

Mother
Home
Friends
You

Prose—

Making the House a Home
My Job As a Father
What My Religion Means to Me
You Can't Live Your Own Life
Why I Go to Church

Why I Go To Church

by

Edgar A Guest

The Reilly & Lee Co.
Chicago   New York

Edgar A. Guest

Contents

Why I Go To Church

I GO to church and contribute to the support of a church because I believe in churches. I would not care to live in a city or a state or a nation in which there were no churches and no churchgoers.

I am not a religious fanatic. I have yet to quarrel with a man regarding his choice of a religion, but I would rather have churchgoers for my neighbors than non-churchgoers.

I would not say that all the good people go to church and that all the bad people stay away from it; but I do say that if my new neighbor has a church affiliation and respects it, the chances are greater that he will be friendly and thoughtful and more considerate of my rights and feelings than would be a non-churchgoer. For the man who assumes that all religion is a mockery and a sham is likely also to assume that all other restraining influences which would interfere with his personal pleasures may be disregarded.

I am not a regular churchgoer in the sense that I attend every Sunday, rain or shine. I do not attend church from a sense of fear or from a sense of duty. I do not believe that God will love all those who go regularly to church, and make outcasts of all those who do not. I believe that the future life is founded on something more liberal and more human than that. I think life on this earth would be intolerable if all had the same opinion and all followed the same rigid course. And I am of the opinion that the fine soul which stays out of the church will be as richly rewarded in the hereafter as the fine soul inside the church.

I have been bored in church. I have been annoyed; I have been made angry; I have encountered in church men for whom I had lost all respect; I have heard things uttered in church which have disgusted me; but I have never lost my faith in the purpose of the church, nor in its ministry as a body. Furthermore, on the whole, I believe in the people who support the church.

ONCE, as a reporter for the Detroit "Free Press," I heard a member of the clergy make this prayer:

"O Lord, put it into the hearts and minds of the people here to give liberally to our support."

I almost laughed in his face. If anything could have driven me away such a prayer as that would have done it. But I didn't blame the church for the foolish man who had strayed into its pulpit.

I am not of the opinion that the church exists to please me. It is here for my guidance and my instruction, for my help and my comfort in times

of sorrow. I do not go to church ex-
pecting to be pampered or praised.
If the minister be worth hearing at
all, I fancy he will now and then
remind me of my shortcomings.

Most folks who have been angered
by ministers have had to listen to
something which they did not like to
hear. The same people hear things
they don't like in theatres, but they
keep right on going to them. They
have been bored by inferior shows;
they have had their intelligence insulted by low comedians who have
sneered at them for their failure to
appreciate their stale jokes; they
have had their pet weaknesses mir-
rored before their eyes; they have
sat with their wives and children and
witnessed obscenity portrayed, but

they continue to help support the theatre.

They have seen bad baseball, and they still go to baseball games.

They have drawn bad cards, but they still play bridge whist.

Business has been bad at times, but they still keep at it and still continue to hope. Friends have cheated them, but they still look to friendship for the lasting joys of life.

The only thing they can't stand for seems to be a minister who doesn't suit their taste. They fail to find perfection in the church, because the sort of perfection they seek is that particular type which agrees entirely with their own notions and conduct in life.

I HAVE only sympathy for the members of the ministry. Theirs is the toughest job I know, bar none. Their work is never done, and, what is more, I fancy it is never done entirely to the satisfaction of all the members of their congregations.

I go to church because I believe in the ministry as a whole. I have never been able to bring myself to believe, as some do, that rector, minister, priest, and rabbi have adopted that profession solely for the salary it pays. You could never convince me that Leo Franklin and Merton Rice and Lynn Hough and Bert Pullinger and Dick Command, and the late beloved Father Van Dyke, all of my town, deliberately elected to become clergymen merely because they thought it an easy and a paying profession.

Father Van Dyke, of St. Aloysius Church, in Detroit, was nearly eighty years of age when he died. If ever a Christlike spirit walked this earth, it was he. The poor knew him better than the rich. His little, old-fashioned down-town home was the calling place for thousands. Everyone who tapped at that door found a friend within. His birthdays were the occasions for the gathering of Protestant and Catholic citizens to do him honor.

I know dozens of men who are giving their lives, as did he, to the service of mankind.

Of course they draw salaries for their toil, but no such salaries as they might draw for such brilliant labor in other fields.

I go to church because I want my children to go to church. I want them to know something more of this life than business and sport. I know only one institution that will teach them that they are divine.

The church will interfere with their pleasures at times, but their mother and I sometimes have to do that, and we hope that they will love us none the less because of it. The church will mystify and puzzle them and seem irksome to them now and then. But all things that are worth while demand something of us in sacrifice. I believe that the church and the things it stands for are necessary to our well-being.

I KNOW that scoffers have become believers, and believers have turned to scoffers, but I cannot bring myself to think that all the millions of people who have given us our churches were fools, and that all the non-believers were wise.

There is room for a difference of opinion; but the man who stays out of church entirely, good citizen though he may be, is leaving to others the care of an institution which makes his neighborhood a safer place for his children to play in.

We are a queer lot about church. We can be married by justices of the peace, but most of us prefer clergymen to tie the knot. We can have our loved ones buried by undertakers, but most of us insist that a clergyman shall say the last sad prayers. In times of sickness and trial and trouble, beyond and above all the assistance of kindly neighbors and friends, we seek the aid and counsel of a minister.

As a reporter, I was a witness to this scene many times:

Someone is dying. The doctors have done all they can do. It is the last hour for a human being.

"Who knows where a minister can be found?" says someone in the room. One is located somewhere, and because the cry comes from the brink of the grave this clergyman answers the call.

"We haven't been churchgoers." sobs the mother, or the wife, or the father, or the son, "and we didn't know whether you'd care to come to us or not, but we'd feel so much better if you'd pray for him and for us."

It is one o'clock in the morning. That clergyman has been roused out of his slumber by total strangers. He strengthens and comforts a passing soul, and sustains for the time being those who remain behind to mourn. They had no use for him yesterday or the day before. But now that they themselves stand in the presence of death, they ask him to come to them and bring with him that faith and comfort which they have never supported, and, it seems, never expected to need.

I GO to church because I believe in it and in its service. When death comes into my home, I shall want a minister whom I have helped and worked with. I shall want to be able to look him in the eyes and greet him without apology. I don't want to say to him: "I have scorned you and your kind and made your works my mockery, but now I need the very thing I have been mocking. I have never given a dollar to the church, but I want the church to bury me."

Most of us are for the church when we are dying. If many of us were not for the church when we are in health, there would be no clergymen to come at our bidding in the last sad hours.

I don't want to beg my prayers at the finish.

I believe that the church is vital to community life. I believe that neither business nor government, nor social service workers, nor any other organization could do the work of the church. A man who has had no religious instruction is not an educated man. We may laugh at the Sunday school, but therein lies the corner-stone of our manhood and womanhood.

God is as much a part of this life as he is of the life to come. I do not vision Him as one dwelling in a far-off place, to be encountered some day as a stern and frowning judge. I believe that much can be learned about Him now. There is a need for religion. Most of us want our children to be trained properly in our faith. Business has no time to teach them; Government has no time to teach religion, nor could it do it wisely if it would, because the paths which lead to God are so many and so varied. This is the proper function of the church and the difficulty now is that the church is struggling to do its duty against terrific odds which we ourselves have raised.

We are all looking to the ministry to give us a finer church. They could do it easily if we would give them a finer and more helpful body of laymen and laywomen.

I go to church and help to support it, not only because I think I need it or may some day need it, but also because I think the church needs me. If all of us who give money thought our duty ended there, the church would die. It exists not on dollars but on men and women.

PERHAPS there are clergymen who have failed to put forth every effort to hold the interest and enthusiasm of their congregations. But it is easy to find an excuse for not going to church.

I myself can always do it. On a lovely June Sunday morning, I much prefer a round of golf to our Episcopal Church service. That God can be worshiped as well under His blue skies and green trees

and on His rolling meadows as
within His dimly lighted building,
I have often said. It is a soothing
balm to my conscience. The only
difficulty about this is that when I
am playing golf on Sunday morning I give little thought to worship.

I can say that the minister doesn't
interest me, and it may be all true,
and it may also be more my fault
than the minister's. If I go to
church only to be interested by an
orator, and not to participate in a
service of worship, then my excuse
for non-attendance is good. But
the fact is that if I am truly sincere
in my church attendance, I can
worship my God in a house con-
ducted by a minister I personally
do not like, just as well as I can

in the presence of one whose elo-
quence both charms and uplifts me.

Regardless of all the costly trap-
pings which have come in to make
churchgoing attractive, the fact re-
mains that we should go for the sake
of worshiping our Creator and
participating in the service of our
own choice. Either we are hypo-
crites or fools when we let one
man's blunder, or one man's arrogance, or one man's intolerance,
drive us away from that one thing
we know to be vital to our peace.

So I continue to go, though I
hear the same things over and over
again better said or worse said by
men I know well and am fond of,
or by men I personally dislike, or
by total strangers.

To say that I don't need the church is mere bravado. I needed it when my father died; I needed it when we were married and when our babies were taken from us, and I shall need it again sooner or later, and need it badly. I am in good health now, and I could, I suppose, get along very nicely for a time without the aid of clergyman, or choir, or even prayer; but what sort of a man is he who scorns and neglects and despises his best friend until his hour of tribulation?

During the summer, which I spend with my family at Pointe Aux Barques, Michigan, I go to church to hear Professor William Lyon Phelps, of Yale University. Born and trained as a Baptist, during the three months of his summer vacation he gives his time and thought and strength to the little Methodist church of Huron City. Every Sunday afternoon he conducts religious services for the benefit of the community at large. For money? No. For publicity? No. For the sake of hearing himself talk? Not at all. It is because he believes in churches and the things for which they stand.

Farmers and summer resorters sit crowded side by side in that little House of God listening to this man's words. They are simple and direct and almost old-fashioned, but they carry with them comfort and hope and faith and courage that could come from no other source than a supreme and abiding faith in

God and Jesus Christ. If Professor Phelps, with all his learning, has found comfort in the things of the Church, who am I to say they are not there?

THE Church is accused of being constantly after money, and I fancy there is a basis for the charge. A more liberal laity could wipe out this degradation.

A constantly begging minister is the living symbol of a niggardly congregation.

I fancy no clergyman enjoys very greatly the money-raising part of his job. A wise and an active vestry or board would save their minister from this humiliation. They would see that the funds necessary for this work were raised for him. They would themselves assume the material burden, and free him for the spiritual work of his parish. In this way, they could make a welcome visitor everywhere instead of a feared and unwelcome one.

The church is an earthly institution. It was built by men to satisfy their spiritual needs. It has been called the House of God, but it is really occupied by human beings, and suffers from every need of human habitation. God does not run the bills or pay them. Men put on the mortgages and men must lift them. Debts can be paid only with money, and money can come only from those who have it. Staying away from church will not lessen its indebtedness. It will only increase it. The difficulty, as I see it, is that now those who do go to church are carrying twice the burden they should. They are maintaining an institution for others who now profess not to need it, but who later on will call upon it for help.

I am inclined to the opinion that as laymen we churchgoers are not all we should be or could be. If the church is not attractive to other people, and especially to young people, we must assume our share of the blame. We cannot in justice shove it all onto the minister. Even the most up-to-date clergyman has to depend upon the old-fashioned Bible and the old-fashioned truths and the old-fashioned faith, for his inspiration and his teaching. It is a church and not a show-house he is conducting. The layman can, by his presence and his support, help make his church an interesting meeting place.

"The people I meet in churches don't interest me," I have heard said countless times. The critics are talking about us churchgoers now. Maybe something is the matter with us. Perhaps we have let our religion make us finicky and super-critical and smug-faced and even hypocritical and bigoted. If our neighbor has no religion of his own, and thinks he wants one, we haven't made him feel that ours is a product to be desired. Apparently it hasn't made us happy and cheerful and helpful and honest and fun-loving. As samples of what our religion does we are all trade killers more or less.

AS a matter of fact, we ourselves aren't convincing in our desire for the church. Of course we go and we pay to its support; but our enthusiasm is not whole-hearted. We're not earnest enough about it. Most of us couldn't convince anyone that the church fills a genuine need in our lives. If this were so, we should be active laymen and laywomen. We should be busy in the church affairs. We should be planners and workers and dreamers for it. At least we should be able to convince our own children that it is a good thing, and even in that most of us seem to fail.

The way to interest young people, and all people, in the church is to make it interesting. How? I think that is the question for the laity to decide. They have established a church for the nurture of the spiritual side of life. They support trained clergymen to preach the gospel and teach the doctrines of their church, but, that done, they have rested. What church members should do is to go out and demonstrate to the world that their religion and their churchgoing make them human and lovable and kind and brave. The wave of doubt which is spreading comes not from the clergy but from the laity.

So I attend church when I can, and do for the church what I can, because I believe in it. I have found nothing in my religion that has interfered with my progress for a single moment. I have never been held back from a single opportunity. It has been my source of inspiration and strength and comfort, and I should be an ingrate and a fool to desert it now. Criticized and derided and belittled, ridiculed and mocked as it is, the Church still stands for all that is finest in our thought. It is still the mother of our greatest sons and daughters.

The Art of Making Friends

The Art of Making Friends

HE WAS a go-getter sales-man.

I sensed that the minute he came into my office. I knew what he was going to say before he had uttered a word of it. And, strangely enough, I knew I was not going to sign on the dotted line for that man. I'd never seen him before, but I didn't like him. However, I let him talk, and the more he talked, the more I disliked him.

In no time at all, I gathered that he was a great salesman. He made no effort whatever to conceal this fact from me. He was once the sales manager for a large concern, so he told me; but he failed to add why he gave up the job. I had my own ideas on the subject.

But in spite of his ability to sell any and everything, he had been a wanderer, going from city to city and from job to job. I learned *that* when he asked me to give him the names of a few of my friends to whom he could present his proposition.

"Any friends of your own here?" I asked.

"No," he said; "you see, I'm so busy doing big things, I don't have much time to make friends. Then, you see, I've changed about so much. You have to be on the go when you're selling."

In other words, this go-getter

salesman could sell anything but himself. He could make stocks and bonds and merchandise attractive to others, but he couldn't make himself attractive. Even if he managed to make a good impression at first, it never lasted after people got to know him. Nobody, it seemed, cared to make any permanent business arrangement with him. He was good enough to sell goods; but he lacked that something which would make you invite him to the house for dinner.

HE HAD the art of salesmanship, but he hadn't the art of making friends.

And the genius for friendship is the greatest of all gifts.

Through one of my clubs passed a citizen of note one day. He has had everything this world can give him—wealth, position, power, respect—but he has few intimate friends. He has never been known to open his heart to another.

He walked through that room, filled with men he knew, as though nobody were there. He recognized a nod of greeting with a nod. He answered every "Hello" that was given to him, but that's all there was to it. If you had been away for six months or more, he would not have gone a step out of his way to welcome you home. Coming face to face with you, perhaps he would express pleasure at seeing you again. But you still would feel

that if he could have passed you
without speaking, he would have
done so. He lacks interest in others.

I've known that man for years. I
know that he values friends, and
that he wishes he had more of them.
But he probably never will, for he
hasn't a genuine interest in people.
It is too late now for him to start
to win them. He has built up for
himself a reputation for coldness
and reserve and indifference. People expect him to be distant. Any
attempt he made to be hail-fellow-
well-met would be looked upon as
insincere.

SOMEBODY got to a man of this
type in a certain big business in
Detroit. He was the millionaire

stockholder who had the last word in the institution. What he said was the law, and everybody about the place knew it. He always had kept himself aloof. Day after day he entered that office without ever saying good morning to anyone.

The meddling somebody told this impersonal employer that he was all wrong. "You ought to be friendlier with the boys and girls in the plant," he said. "It would do you and them a lot of good if you walked among them occasionally and talked to them. They're all afraid of you. They think you're the Big Bear that is ready to gobble them up."

"I've never had the knack of making friends," said he, "and I'm sorry I've given the wrong impression. I'll try my best to treat the boys a little better from now on."

He started the very next morning. As he stepped into the elevator, he noticed in the car the foreman of one of the departments.

"Good morning, Jim," he said. "This is a beautiful day."

The reply was not what he expected.

Jim looked him straight in the eyes and said:

"Mr. ——, I've worked for this institution a little over twenty-five years now, and I've done fairly well for the company and my family without ever having you say 'Good morning' to me. You don't need to start now." With that he stepped out of the car and went to his work.

It was too late. You can't slight a man for twenty-five years, and then decide to turn over a new leaf and greet him like a brother. You may mean to be friendly, but the other man will suspect your motive.

The comedian may long to play Hamlet, but the public won't have it. The tragedian may think he can do a better song-and-dance act than the vaudeville artist does; but the managers know better than to let him try.

To have friends, a man must first be a friend. He who has many friends has been a friend to many.

The art of friendship is self-acquired. Men go to schools to learn to paint, and carve, and draw, and write; there are dancing-schools and finishing-schools for girls where etiquette and deportment are taught for a price; there are correspondence schools for many crafts and many arts; but the greatest of all the arts—that of making friends —comes to a man from within, and only when he makes patient effort to deserve it.

Friendship must be a lifetime habit. The most important thing you can teach a boy is how to get along with his fellows. Nature, I suppose, has something to do with our likes and dislikes; our strengths and weaknesses. But the control of our conduct is in our own hands. He who comes to the end of life's road with no devoted friends has only himself to blame.

I have in mind a man in Detroit who is liked by all who know him. Even men he has discharged from his employ still cherish his friendship.

He hasn't found it necessary to sacrifice discipline to be kindly. He can run his business well, and still be human.

I was riding with him one day when he suddenly swerved his car off the main street.

"Do you mind going a few blocks out of the way?" he said. "It just occurred to me that I ought to make a stop on the way out."

In a few minutes, we were in a section of town inhabited by foreign workmen. The cottages looked all alike.

"Here's the place I'm looking for," he said and stopped. "I won't be a minute."

I NOTICED crape on the door which he was approaching. He had said nothing to me of his mission, but when he came out he remarked:

"I'm glad I did that. I hope you didn't mind waiting."

"Someone in trouble?" I asked.

"Yes," he said. "We've had a young Pole working in our foundry for the past three or four years, a good, clean, honest, hard-working boy. I liked his manner the first time I saw him, and when I go through the plant, I usually stop to talk to him. I always get a laugh out of his quaint expressions. You know you really get to like those boys. His baby died yesterday. The firm sent out a few flowers, but I thought I'd stop by myself and see if there was anything I could do."

"And was there anything you could do?" I asked.

"No, not a thing," he replied. "He had saved up some money, and everything's all right so far as the finances are concerned. But it seemed to cheer him up a lot to have me walk into his house. His wife kissed my hand and he introduced me to his people as 'the boss.' I couldn't understand a word they said, but I got enough to know how glad he was to know that I had called on him as his friend."

They don't teach that sort of
thing in schools. That's inside art.
That's friendship as practiced by
one who knows what real friendship means. That millionaire employer went to the little cottage as
the friend of a Polish father. I can
reconstruct that scene. He talked
to those grief-stricken parents simply and earnestly. There was no
distinction then of head-office and
foundry. They were all in the presence of death and the big man was
helpless to change that situation,
and he knew it. All his money and
all his pride and all his power could
do nothing. He probably put his
arm about that suffering father and
uttered what few words of consola-
tion he could think to say. When

he was being introduced to the strange friends of that family, he displayed no sense of superiority. I'll wager all I have that he made those people feel he was glad and proud to meet them. He was a friend of the family, and friends are friends whether they live in cottages or mansions.

WHY is it some people are liked and others greatly disliked? It is not altogether a question of honesty and fair dealing. Apparently it has nothing to do with respectability, for many respectable people are not popular. It seems to me to be wholly a matter of manners, and manners are usually prompted by the heart.

Analyzing the various people who seem always to annoy me and "get on my nerves" is not difficult. Some of them are boastful. They walk the world with a superior air; they are forever mentioning their possessions; they are always talking of people "who are beneath their notice." In a world so crowded, they would give you the idea that only they and a very few others are really worth while.

There are others who are flagrantly selfish in little things. They are openly bad-mannered. They want all the advantages. They are the elbowers in the crowd; the road hogs on the street; the rushers for first place at the dining table.

Another type I don't like is sim-

ply malicious. Persons of this class
have bitter tongues and cruel minds.
Their jests always carry a sting.
They seem to lie in wait for you to
spring the one sentence which they
know will hurt you most. You can
never be comfortable in their presence. Play host to one of these, and
your party is dancing on dynamite.
Sooner or later one of your guests
is going to be insulted or slurred,
for the poisoned tongue knows no
law of hospitality or friendship or
courtesy.

The two-faced man or woman is
difficult to endure. This type leaves
a trail of broken confidences behind
it. It plies you with intimate ques-
tions, only to broadcast the in-
formation where it will do you the

most harm. It is the sneak-thief of social life. It is false to all and true to none, and the only good thing about it is that it can so easily and quickly be detected and so simply guarded against. Unpopularity and isolation are its rewards.

Churlish people are unpopular everywhere. So are people filthy both of person and of speech. Nobody long enjoys the company of the loud and flashy person, or of the morose and crabbed. The flatterer falls on the rocks of insincerity, and the liar and the cheat are soon discarded by society.

The art of making friends lies in knowing how to avoid these dangers. It seems to me that he who would properly equip his boy or girl for life in this world should begin early with the teaching of manners.

Is an ill temper admired by anyone? Not at all. Then put away your silly fits of rage. Do you like the lad who cheats to win? You don't? Then never be a cheat yourself. Do you like to hear slurs and sneers and smart words that sting and burn? No. Then think twice before you utter them. Do you like to be warmly welcomed? Do you like to receive the little attentions which are evidences of thoughtfulness and respect for you? You do. Then bestow them always on others, particularly on those who may not rightfully expect them. This is the road to friendship.

The art of making friends is not difficult. The ways of people we like and love are not difficult to understand. There is nothing mysterious about them. They sigh when they are in trouble and they groan when they are hurt. They suffer disappointment and grief and loss. In every human way they are just like us—and yet they are different. And it is that difference which draws us to them.

There is a man of many friends in Detroit. He is still a young man. He is an outstanding business success; but above and beyond that shines his personal success. His presence radiates good feeling and good will. I have never heard the poorest man envy him his good fortune. The richest in town delight in his friendship. What is his secret? He hasn't any. The friends of his boyhood are his friends today. Drive up to his house in pride and arrogance, seeking to share in his power and glory, and what will you find? Arrogance and Pomp enthroned to greet you?

Not at all. You'll receive a duplicate of the welcome just given to the humbler friends who preceded you. He'll come to the door with a smile and a handshake and a word of delight for your coming. After that he will take you into that spacious living-room and introduce you to the friends of the family. Maybe you will find a friend of his boyhood, who now clerks in your

store. At any rate you'd better leave
any snobbishness or false pride at
home.

I WAS there once when the house
was new. An old couple, friends
of his mother, who was still living
with him, called. Never could roy-
alty have received a warmer welcome. Those two lovely old people
were plainly ill at ease. Perhaps in
all their lives they had never before
entered a rich man's house. They
had known their host as a boy and
had been friends with him, but he
had gone up in the world and they
had remained where he left them.
No wonder they felt a little uncer-
tain of their welcome.

But not for long. The dear old

lady was almost swept off her feet by a hug which that great big boy gave her, and the little old man got a handshake which he'll never forget.

Proudly the young host introduced them to all of us. And then, turning to his two elderly visitors, he said, "Wouldn't you like to see the house?" Would they? They were itching to see it—every inch of it, from cellar to attic.

"Excuse me a few minutes," the boy said to the rest of us. "You folks have been all over the place, but I do want these friends of mine to see it."

I went along. In less time than it takes to tell, the guests of honor were perfectly at home. The little old lady was feeling tapestries and curtains and silk bed coverings and reveling in their beauty. And the old man was chattering of by-gone days when the boy didn't have so much. They laughed together and they sighed together, and later they drank a little wine together for old time's sake.

They were no longer afraid of soiling new carpets and new curtains. There was no chasm between them and their host which he wouldn't help them across. He hadn't forgotten them. He was rich; but he was still the same, lovable, happy-hearted boy who once sat at the table in their cottage. He was as fond of them as ever. They didn't have to be told that.

It's an art to be able to make people happy. It's an art to be genuine and real and solid and worth-while. It's an art to dismiss everything that is petty and trivial and insignificant, and play the host and friend. Making friends is an art. Keeping them is a greater one.

And that is why everybody likes this man I've been telling you about. He has never discharged a friend as being no longer worth his notice.

NOT long ago, he and I were discussing a man we both know—a chap who apparently had cut away all the old ties and was seeking new alliances that would help him up the social ladder.

"It will never work," my wise
young friend said. "He's going
wrong, as wrong as the man who
takes to drink. Money has spoiled
him. He has begun to strut, and
strutting is bad manners. He never
sees his old friends any more.
That's worse than bad manners.
No man is so rich that he can afford
to throw away a friend."

Oh, boy of mine, I saw you yesterday on the golf course and was
proud of you. You had your arm
about your caddie's shoulders You
were the employer and he was the
workman. Chance had made it pos-
sible for you to play golf and
chance had cast that lad for the
role of your caddie. The two of
you were laughing your way along

that course, comrades in the game. I saw you, and I rejoiced in the sight.

Keep that attitude to the end of the road. Never give up a friend. One you think your friend may give you up; but let the fault be his, and his the loss. Never spoil your life by boasting. Confidence in yourself is one thing, but a haughty and overbearing manner is another. Take a lesson from your hero, Lindbergh. He went to New York a stranger, unannounced. To a few he was known as one of the flying group. He did no boasting in advance. He merely said that he had come to attempt the flight to Paris. Quietly he set about his plans. And then one morning, the whole world

knew that Lindbergh was on the
way.

"Lindbergh has reached Paris!"
came the cabled word.

"Who is this Lindbergh?" asked
the world.

To-day everybody in the world
knows who Lindbergh is. Achieve-
ment is its own mouthpiece.

FORGET yourself. Think of
others. Know what your rights
are, and then forget most of them.

Herein lies friendship.

The art of making friends con-
sists in doing graciouly and quickly
and cheerfully the things which
will make others happy.

What is it we like in our friends?
I think it is their understanding of

us. They are familiar with our whims and fancies and shortcomings. They graciously accommodate themselves to us. That's why we cling to them. They have the power to wound and cut us to the quick, but they never do it. When they do remind us of our faults they do it with sympathy and not with ridicule. So we hold fast to them, and love them and struggle to be like them.

Well, boy of mine, the men and women out in the big, busy, crowded world are much like us. They want to be liked. They are sensitive to injury and to slight. They detest boastful people. They like attention from others. Little favors please them. A glad "Good morning" is sweet music to their ears and a smiling face delights them.

If you understand this and remember it, the art of making friends will become yours. Say to yourself as the stranger approaches, "Here is one I have never before seen. I don't know his name or his mission or his occupation.

Then if you treat him as you would yourself want to be treated, he'll go on his way saying to himself, "Well, at that spot I met a real fellow."

Look the crowd over again, son! You are going out in it soon. You told me just the other day about a boy who is always bragging, and you told me how the other boys dislike him for it. The crowd hates liars and cheats. Some of them may be liars and cheats themselves, but if you become one they'll hate you for it.

There's no secret about that throng. Every single one of them respects manhood; likes good nature; admires sportsmanship; and loves the decent things. They may not all do the decent thing themselves; but if you are fair and clean and kindly they'll recognize the fact and respect you for it.

There they are, millions and millions of them, men and women just like you and me and your mother and your sister. They reverence the same flag and they worship the same God. There are many creeds among them; but friends are the common need of them all.

THE art of making friends—is the art of being a gentleman. You'll never make a mistake if you treat the worst woman in the lot as though she were a lady, and the worst man as though he were a brother.

You can't know everybody. Even in a long and crowded lifetime, you can become a close friend to only a few. But thousands will cross your path. Many you may see only for a minute, or an hour, or a day. But when you have gone your separate ways somebody has taken your measure.

You know the difference between

"Good morning" and a grunt. So do the people you encounter during a day. Does the barber who cuts your hair try to do his best for you? If he doesn't, perhaps it's a proof that you haven't tried to show your best side to the barber. If he likes you, he'll try to please you. If he dislikes you, he won't. That's your way with people you like and with people you dislike. It's my way; it's everybody's way.

The man who has many friends has been a friend to many. He has understood the needs of many. He has known, without being told, that other people like to have attention shown to them, and he has shown that attention graciously and gracefully. He has slighted no man needlessly.

He has walked the earth with all men as one of them. He has understood the need of all for laughter. The fellowship of joy and grief has been an open book to him. The chances are he has suffered sorrow, and he knows how deeply grief cuts, and he remembers when another is in trouble.

We have different tastes and habits and customs and fancies, but in the main touches of life we are all alike. Birth, death, christenings, graduation, marriage, and again birth and the same round of joy and heartaches—make up the sum of human living. We never grow too great to be above and beyond these things. We never reach a point where we have no need of friends.

Printed in the United States
217451BV00001BA/3/A